GREAT BUILDINGS

THE EMPIRE STATE BUILDING

Gini Holland

RSVP
RAINTREE
STECK-VAUGHN
P U B L I S H E R S
The Steck-Vaughn Company

Austin, Texas

GREAT BUILDINGS

THE COLOSSEUM

THE EMPIRE STATE BUILDING

THE GREAT PYRAMID

THE HOUSES OF PARLIAMENT

THE PARTHENON

THE TAJ MAHAL

Published by Raintree Steck-Vaughn Publishers,
an imprint of Steck-Vaughn Company

Library of Congress Cataloging-in-Publication Data
Holland, Gini.
The Empire State Building / Gini Holland.
    p.   cm.—(Great buildings)
    Includes bibliographical references and index.
    Summary: Chronicles the building of the world famous skyscraper, describes its occupants, and explores its popularity in films.
    ISBN 0-8172-4919-2
    1. Empire State Building (New York, N.Y.)—Juvenile literature. 2. New York (N.Y.)—Buildings, structures, etc.—Juvenile literature.
    [1. Empire State Building (New York, N.Y.). 2. Buildings. 3. Skyscrapers. 4. New York (N.Y.)—Buildings, structures, etc.]
    I. Title. II. Series.
    F128.8.E46H65   1997
    974.7'1—dc21   96-52800

Printed in Italy. Bound in the United States.
1 2 3 4 5 6 7 8 9 0 02 01 00 99 98

Illustrations: Mick Gillah
Maps: Peter Bull

CONTENTS

▼ The movie *King Kong* was made soon after the Empire State Building was built. Since then, New York City's famous landmark has appeared in many other films.

"THE MOST AWESOME THRILLER OF ALL TIME"
the one and only

KING KONG

with
FAY WRAY
ROBT. ARMSTRONG
BRUCE CABOT

ON TOP OF THE WORLD

King Kong stands on top of the Empire State Building, gripping the dome with his feet. Airplanes buzz all around him, firing and swerving away. The year is 1933. The Empire State Building, tallest building in the world, is just two years old. As the cameras continue to roll, the giant ape is hit and roars with pain. He grabs at an airplane and crumples it in one huge, hairy paw.

The pilots zoom in and fire again. King Kong reels and loses his balance. He slips and falls, bouncing hard against the building. He keeps falling, bounces again as the building widens out, and still he falls, until he crashes onto the street. The crowds gather around his huge body, which fills the intersection of 34th Street and Fifth Avenue in the heart of New York City.

CHAPTER ONE

THE LAND OF OPPORTUNITY

This painting shows New York around 1650, when the first Dutch immigrants had begun to settle. They called it New Amsterdam, and it was only when the English took control in 1664 that it became New York.

The city that provided the setting for King Kong's great dramatic moment began very modestly. New York City has a great natural harbor, so it was one of the first landing places for European immigrants. They came to find a better life in what is now the United States of America. The Dutch and English set up settlements on Manhattan Island, forcing out the Algonquian Indians who were living there. Other early immigrants came against their will, brought as slaves from Africa.

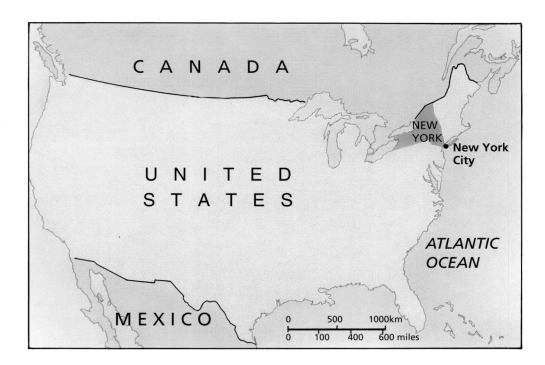

▶ You can see where New York City is situated on this map of the United States.

New York became the capital of the United States for a brief period, from 1785 to 1790. President George Washington was inaugurated there on April 30, 1789. By the following year, New York City had 33,000 inhabitants and was the largest city in the U.S.

In 1799, an Englishman named John Thompson bought an uncultivated piece of land on Manhattan for $2,600. He farmed the land for 25 years, as the city to the south of him continued to grow. The immigrants continued to arrive, and within ten years the population of New York City had almost doubled.

◀ The island of Manhattan, where the Empire State Building stands, was originally inhabited by the Canarsees tribe of the Algonquian Indians. This 18th-century woodcut shows how the Europeans viewed New York's original inhabitants.

More people poured in each year, and many were willing to pay a high price for land near the harbor. This was where the boats came in, goods were traded, and money was made. Thompson sold his farm in 1825 for $10,000. Two years later, it was sold to William Backhouse Astor for $20,500.

By 1862, the Astor family had built two mansions on the site of the Thompson farm. William Waldorf Astor then demolished one of the mansions and erected the Waldorf Hotel, which opened in 1893.

The city itself was changing fast. After 1898, it included not only Manhattan but the boroughs of Brooklyn, the Bronx, Queens, and Staten Island. By 1900, the population had grown to almost three and a half million. Immigrants had arrived from countries such as Ireland,

▲ A postcard from 1860 shows how the island of Manhattan and its neighboring districts were beginning to look like a city as immigrants continued to arrive in large numbers.

Germany, Poland, and Italy, setting up their own neighborhoods. They brought different languages, foods, traditions, and religions, helping to make New York the multicultural city it is today.

◀ The Statue of Liberty was placed in New York harbor in 1886. For generations of immigrants arriving by ship, it was a symbol of hope and opportunity.

▲ After 1865, Jewish immigrants started to arrive in New York from eastern Europe. This photograph, taken around 1900, shows Hester Street market on the bustling Lower East Side.

Although World War I (1914–18) was a great tragedy for the world, it gave a major boost to the American economy. After the war ended American farmers sold food to Europe at good prices. Many spent their profits on new cars, appliances, and homes. All this spending created jobs in manufacturing for returning soldiers and many others.

In January 1920, a new Prohibition law took effect, banning the production and sale of alcohol. Demand for alcohol immediately went up, and crooks and gangsters across the country got rich by selling alcohol illegally. The war was over, jobs were plentiful, and people wanted to celebrate. While the Roaring Twenties lasted, people had money to spend. Wall Street in downtown Manhattan was the financial center of the United States, where fortunes were made and lost overnight.

▼ During Prohibition, alcohol was made and sold illegally all over the United States. These Federal agents have discovered a still that was used for just this purpose.

◄ The Waldorf-Astoria, New York's largest hotel, was demolished in October 1929.

Two things remained constant in New York City: population growth and land price increases. The Waldorf Hotel had merged with a new building on the site of its neighboring Astor mansion in 1897, to become the Waldorf-Astoria. In 1928 the hotel was sold for about $16 million. It was soon demolished to make way for the Empire State Building. The land had changed from a farm to a huge hotel to a hole in the ground in a little more than a century, but its price had gone in only one direction: up.

CHAPTER TWO

THE BIRTH OF SKYSCRAPERS

▼ When an inner steel frame (1) was used, outside walls didn't have to be so thick. This meant that buildings could go higher without collapsing. Strong foundations (2) underground helped support the steel structure above.

As American cities grew more and more crowded, shortage of space became a problem. Because of this, buildings had to go up rather than across. Skyscrapers were the solution to this space problem.

The key to making buildings taller was to use an inner supporting frame so that their outer walls didn't have to bear all the weight. These frames were made possible by inventions that had already taken place. Around the mid-1800s, the use of cast-iron posts and beams to support large buildings became widespread. By 1865, Henry Bessemer had perfected the process of making steel from iron and other elements. Steel is four to five times stronger than iron, and twenty

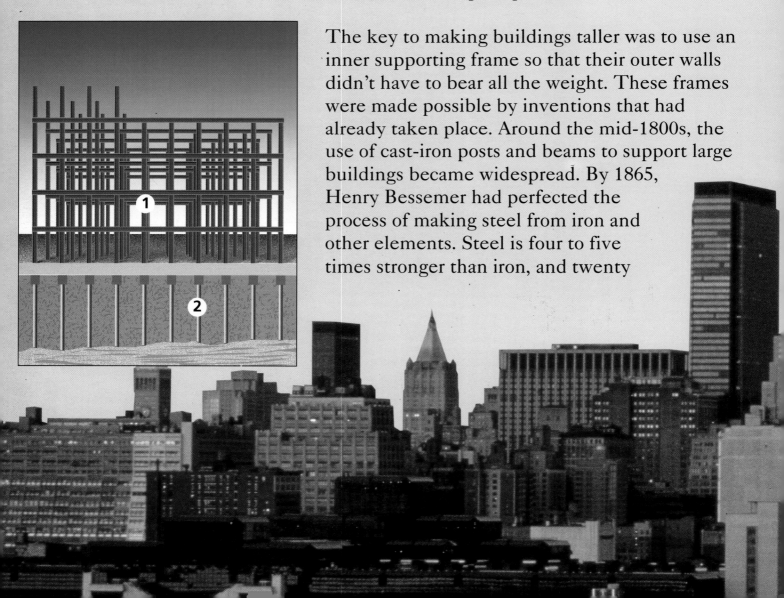

times stronger than wood. With steel frames to support walls, floors, and roofs, people were able to build higher and higher.

As their buildings got bigger and more complicated, architects needed to work with structural engineers to make sure that what they were planning would stand up to high winds, gravity, and time. Teams of experts, including architects, builders, plumbers, electricians, and engineers, had to pool their efforts and work together. Certain construction workers also offered a vital skill: many Native Americans performed the highest and most dangerous tasks, appearing to have no fear of heights.

▲ In the past 120 years, Chicago's skyscrapers have led the way for other cities. The Home Insurance Building was the first in the United States built with an all-metal frame and steel beams. Erected in 1885, it was the forerunner of modern skyscrapers.

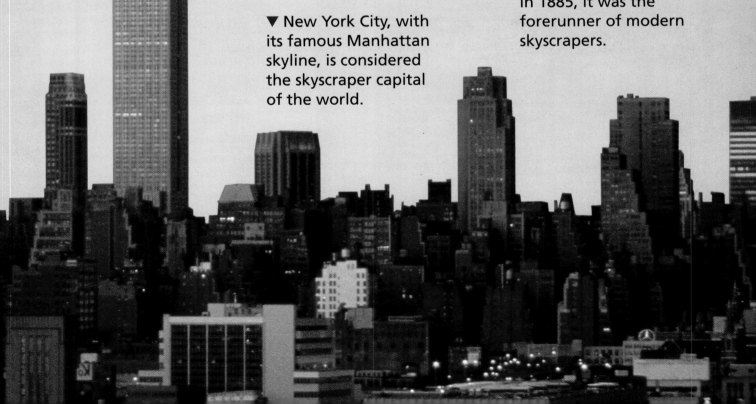

▼ New York City, with its famous Manhattan skyline, is considered the skyscraper capital of the world.

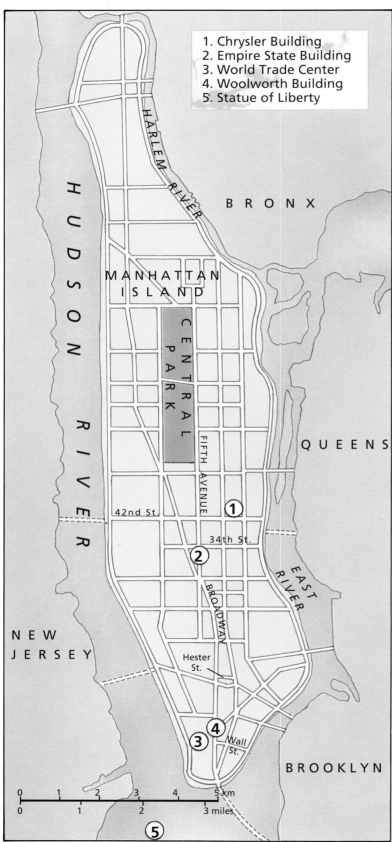

1. Chrysler Building
2. Empire State Building
3. World Trade Center
4. Woolworth Building
5. Statue of Liberty

◄ Manhattan is a long narrow island running north to south between the East River and the Hudson River in the heart of New York City. The Empire State Building still dominates a forest of skyscrapers in the city's shopping district.

► The neo-Gothic Woolworth Building looms elegantly over City Hall Park. The world's tallest building from 1914 to 1929, it was designed by Cass Gilbert and has 60 floors.

Getting to the top
Another invention was essential if people were to live and work in skyscrapers. Reliable elevators were needed, because people were not going to climb more than ten floors, let alone 70, to get to their office! In 1852 the first safety device for elevators was designed by Elisha Otis. It prevented elevators from plunging down their shafts if their cables broke. Otis elevators, powered by steam, were installed in skyscrapers until electric elevators took over in the 1900s.

▼ The most distinctive and beautiful spire in New York City, with its overlapping plates resembling car wheels, is that of the Chrysler Building, designed by William van Alen. It has 77 floors and stands 1,046 ft. (319 m) high.

As the population of New York City continued to grow, along with the city's importance as a financial center, the need for office space also grew. This in turn raised the price of property. The expansion of the city's economy, especially in the 1920s, created demand for more efficient use of ground. These factors led to the construction of almost two hundred skyscrapers between 1902 and 1929.

The Woolworth Building, at 790 ft. (241 m), became the world's tallest building in 1914. It was overtaken in 1929 by the Bank of Manhattan, and then in 1930 by the Chrysler Building. The reign of the Chrysler Building was brief. Neighboring ground was already being prepared for the Empire State Building.

CHAPTER THREE

THE PLAN FOR THE BUILDING

▼ Alfred E. Smith (1873-1944), four times elected governor of New York, was one of the city's most popular and well-known figures.

The two men who decided to build the tallest building in the world had never built anything before.

In 1928 Alfred E. Smith, the governor of New York, was chosen by the Democratic Party to run for president of the United States. John J. Raskob, national chairman of the Democratic Party, had been a top executive at General Motors. Smith needed Raskob's money and business connections during the election, and thus chose him to manage the presidential campaign.

Smith campaigned to stop businesses from making children work long hours for very little money and to pay compensation to workers laid off from their jobs. During the prosperous 1920s, most people didn't see the need for these changes. The election was won instead by the Republican candidate Herbert Hoover. Meanwhile, Franklin D. Roosevelt had taken over as governor of New York,

◀ John Jacob Raskob, the self-made millionaire who led the Empire State Building investors. Asked by Smith to help run his presidential campaign, he in turn employed Smith as the front man for the Empire State Building.

and Smith was out of a job. Raskob was in the same boat: General Motors had asked him to resign when he became chairman of the Democratic Party.

Both men were looking for something to do. They decided to build an office building that would rival the Chrysler Building (the Chrysler car company was General Motors' main competitor). Raskob would use his money to get it started, and they would raise money from other investors, such as Pierre du Pont, to build the tallest building in the world.

"Anyone not only can be rich but ought to be rich."

John Raskob

▶ This front page headline appeared in the *New York Times* on August 30, 1929.

SMITH TO HELP BUILD HIGHEST SKYSCRAPER

Ex-Governor Heads Group That Will Put 80-Story Office Building on Waldorf Site.

COST PUT AT $60,000,000

He Will Be President and Have Executive Control of Concern Yet to Be Incorporated.

Former Governor Alfred E. Smith will head a company to be incorporated to build the highest building in the world on the site of the Waldorf-Astoria Hotel. The structure, to be known as the Empire State Building, will be an office building, eighty stories high, and will cost, with the $16,000,000 paid for the site, more than $60,000,000. It will occupy more than two acres of land with 200 feet on Fifth Avenue and 425 feet on Thirty-third and Thirty-fourth Streets.

Mr. Smith, who will be president of the Empire State Building Corporation, made the announcement in his suite at the Hotel Biltmore in accordance with a promise made months ago to newspaper reporters that he would announce his business plans as soon as he had determined them. The former Governor said that supervision of the construction of the building and its management would be his main business. Since his retirement from the Governorship Mr. Smith has been elected a director of the Metropolitan Life Insurance Company and the New

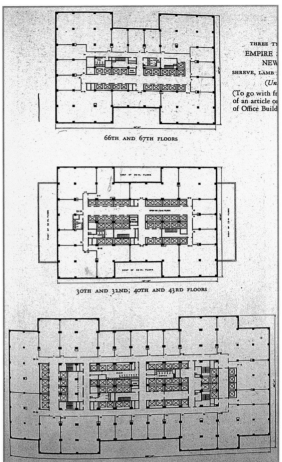

THREE TY
EMPIRE :
NEW
SHREVE, LAMB :
(Un
(To go with fr
of an article or
of Office Build

66TH AND 67TH FLOORS

30TH AND 32ND; 40TH AND 43RD FLOORS

▲ This architect's
drawing shows the
floor plan for three
levels of the Empire
State Building. All
the offices were
on the outside, for
maximum light and
space, while the
central core was for
elevators, stairwells,
and utilities.

▶ William Lamb, the Empire State
Building's architect, was noted for his
sober designs. He followed current
styles, but disliked some of New York's
more flamboyant architecture.

"Our plan is to find the best available brains...in various branches of engineering, in architecture, building and labor. Then we will put all our ideas on the table. The best of the ideas...are the ones we will use."

Robert Shreve, of Shreve, Lamb, and Harmon, 1929

Smith and Raskob knew they wanted something big, but they didn't care about beauty or design. They left that to their architects. They hired the firm of Shreve, Lamb, and Harmon, and William F. Lamb was put in charge of the project. His design was partly influenced by the perpendicular style of another architect, Eliel Saarinen.

Lamb's wife has said since that her husband based most of his design on a simple pencil. "The clean soaring lines inspired him, and he modeled the building after it."

Lamb had to follow certain regulations when he was deciding on the shape of the building. The zoning laws for Manhattan said tall buildings had to get smaller as they went up so that they didn't block all the air and light from neighboring buildings. So Lamb designed a five-story base that filled the whole site and lined up with the buildings already there. He topped it with setbacks, or floors that were set back from the base.

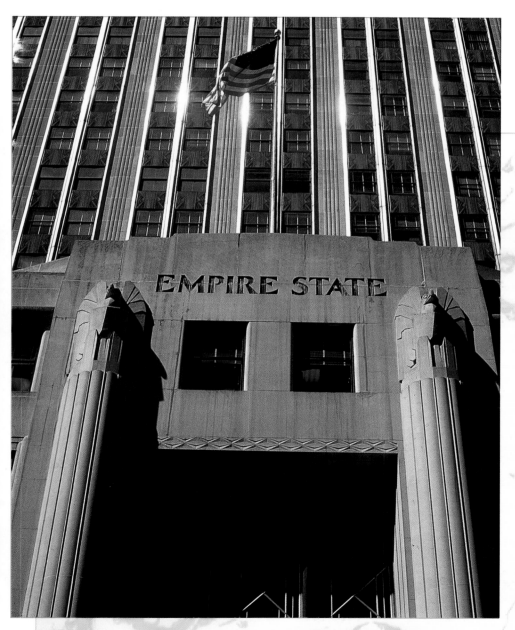

Art Deco
The decorative style of the Empire State Building followed the fashion of the 1920s and 1930s. This was a style that was later named Art Deco—at the time it was known as "Art Moderne," or even "Skyscraper Modern." The distinctive geometric and curved shapes of the style were seen in buildings, furniture, jewelry, and textiles from about 1910 to 1940. The Empire State Building is a modest example of Art Deco, with little exterior detail and restrained interior decoration.

The future of the Empire State Building was suddenly thrown into doubt by a huge financial crisis. The Wall Street Crash of October 1929 came about in a wave of panic. Wall Street was home to the New York Stock Exchange, where people could make money by buying and selling shares, or stocks, in businesses. The panic came when these investors all lost faith in the stock market at the same time. The effect of everybody selling at once was to make their shares almost worthless. Most investors lost their fortunes.

Because of the crisis, businesses failed all over the country, and many people lost their jobs. They could no longer buy goods and services, so the companies that provided them began to go bankrupt, too, and had to let their workers go. The cycle of poverty known as the Great Depression began.

▼ In October 1929 Wall Street was filled with investors desperate to recoup their money by selling their shares. With everybody selling, there was of course nobody to buy, except at rock bottom prices.

Luckily, Raskob had been careful with his money, and was able to turn the Depression to his advantage. The cost of employing people fell drastically. So many people needed jobs that it was easy to find laborers to work long and hard for low wages. Because of the Depression, the cost of building the Empire State Building, at under $25 million, was half of what Smith and Raskob had expected.

◀ During the Great Depression, long lines of people waiting for cheap food or the chance of a job were a frequent sight. The offer of a meal at the "One Cent" restaurant in New York attracted hundreds of hungry people.

CHAPTER FOUR

THE BUILDING GOES UP

From October 1929 to February 1930, demolition workers were busy pulling down and removing the old hotel on the Empire State Building site. Sixteen thousand truckloads of rubble were taken away and deposited at sea.

▼ At the beginning of 1930, excavation work was underway. A temporary structure around the site formed a safe walkway for passersby, with offices above. In the shadow on the left you can see the shapes of two derricks, used for lifting heavy loads.

◀ Smith laid the building's original cornerstone on September 17, 1930. A crowd of 5,000 people, including workers on the building, gathered as he cemented the huge stone into place with a silver trowel. Smith became an honorary member of the Bricklayers' Union in order to perform this task.

On January 22, 1930, excavation of the site began. This involved digging down 35 ft. (10.6 m) with steam shovels to prepare the site for foundations. Excavation also produced a staggering amount of waste. It is estimated that the earth and rock removed were nearly as heavy as the completed building (which weighed 365,000 tons when finished in 1931).

Shifts of men worked around the clock. While parts of the site were still being excavated, other teams were already laying foundations. The steel and concrete foundations were secured by footings embedded in rock 55 ft. (17 m) below ground level. The foundations would support the structure and distribute the weight of the huge building that was to rise above them.

"Six hundred men, working day and night in shifts of 300, have made the excavations, among them eighty drill runners. Four steam shovels have been used, as well as three cranes, three derricks, four air compressors, and two blacksmith shops."

From the *New York Times*, March 6, 1930

A near-strike at the Empire State

Organizations that protected the rights of workers, called unions, were especially important to workers during the Depression, when employers could take advantage of people's desperation for jobs. In April 1930, building workers at the Empire State Building called for a strike because their employers were using workers who weren't union members and were willing to work for less money. Smith met with union representatives all day on April 5. They agreed to a settlement, and the strike was avoided.

An average of 2,500 people per day worked on the construction of the Empire State Building. From the time construction began on March 17, 1930, the building's steel frame rose at an average rate of four and a half floors per week. During one ten-day period alone, the building jumped fourteen floors. To speed construction, the building's posts, beams, windows, and window frames were made in factories and put together on the site.

◄ Workers using a huge derrick guide a steel girder into place. Girders, beams, and posts formed the framework of the entire building.

Some 60,000 tons of steel were brought in from the steel mills of Pittsburgh, Pennsylvania, 310 mi. (500 km) away. The steel had already been made into parts such as the immensely strong I-beams and H-beams, shaped like their names. The beams were brought by train, barge, and truck to the site and could be installed within three and a half days of being made.

The construction workers used a fast, assembly-line approach to building. Lifting crews, using derricks and other hoists, raised the steel into position. The high-iron workers fitted everything together, and the riveting gangs followed on to fasten the steel in place. The men moved up, making self-contained boxes over and over again. By July 1930, they were constructing the frame of the 40th floor.

◄ A lifting gang at work on the lower floors of the Empire State Building. Teamwork was an essential part of the incredibly fast construction methods used on the skyscraper.

▲ This photograph was taken on July 21, 1930, when work had begun on the 40th floor.

As the building climbed higher, the men and materials were carried up in elevators. The derricks were in constant use, swinging the heaviest parts to higher and higher levels. A miniature railroad was built at each level to carry supplies. A timetable was issued every day, showing what was going up in the elevators and where it would be taken by the little trains.

Five mobile cafeterias went up and down the scaffolding, bringing sandwiches, pies, coffee, and milk. Drinking water was piped to the

▼ High above the city, a workman takes a break, apparently unconcerned by his precipitous position. As the building grew, workers found themselves opening their lunchboxes in the clouds.

◄ A riveting team at work. You can see the rivet being heated below, the catcher waiting above with his bucket, and the bucker-up working on the beam at the top.

workers through 10 mi. (16 km) of water pipes. A hospital with an emergency room and a full staff of doctors and nurses was set up on the ground floor to take care of accidents.

The danger involved in working so high up was breathtaking. In the 1930s, safety equipment was scarce, and fourteen people lost their lives during the Empire State Building's construction.

In addition to the height, tools and materials also posed dangers. Teams of riveters had the job of joining the frame together. The first member of the team heated a rivet to red-hot and then used tongs to throw it to a catcher with a bucket. It was passed to the bucker-up to insert into the frame, where the riveter flattened it in place as it fused the metal parts together.

▼ By October 3, 1930, there were 88 floors finished and only another 14 to go.

The economy had crashed, but the Empire State Building zoomed up like a rocket. As well as the frame, the outer walls of the Empire State Building went up at record speed.

Lamb decided that columns of stone would be easy to put up if they were separated from the windows with metal strips. The strips covered the stone's edges, which meant the stone could be rough-cut at the quarry and then heaved into place without any final cutting or fitting. The stonework, started in June 1930, was completed in November. The windows were attached with metal brackets between the stone columns, with aluminum panels above and below each level.

▼ Nearly to the top: a sky boy, as the highest workers were known, swings over New York on a rope.

▶ Two men at the topmost level, working on the dome.

▼ This picture of the Empire State Building clearly shows the separate strips forming outer walls. Placing metal between the windows and the stonework allowed the glass and stone crews to work at their own pace. If one crew worked slowly, the other could move ahead.

The owners had declared "What this building needs is a hat!" As a result, the top 15 floors took the form of a distinctive tower of glass, steel, and aluminum. Originally intended as a mooring mast for airships, the tower was about 200 ft. (60 m) high and topped with a dome.

Inside the building, meanwhile, other people were hard at work. Concrete was poured into place for the floors, and interior brick walls were constructed. Stairways and elevator shafts were installed, as were many miles of pipes and cables. There was a lot of work to be done to finish the building by the deadline of May 1, 1931.

The Empire State Building took only one year and 45 days to build, or 7 million man hours. This is still a record for a skyscraper of such a height. When it was completed, it stood 1,250 ft. (381 m) high. It had been given the name for the state of New York, "the Empire State," and was soon to become the symbol for New York City.

Set in the center of the building, the elevators and their shafts took up almost a third of the floor space. The original 67 elevators were designed to travel at about 985 ft. (300 m) a minute.

An observation deck had been placed on the 86th floor, 1,050 ft. (320 m) up, from which visitors could see for 40 mi. (64 km). From the 102nd floor, where there is now a second observatory, it is possible on a clear day to see for 80 mi. (128 km).

◀ The marble for the lavish entrance lobby was quarried from all over Europe. The contents of one entire quarry were used to make sure the color and grain would match perfectly.

▶ The Empire State Building, as it was when it was finished in 1931. Parts of the building are cut away in this picture to show the inside.

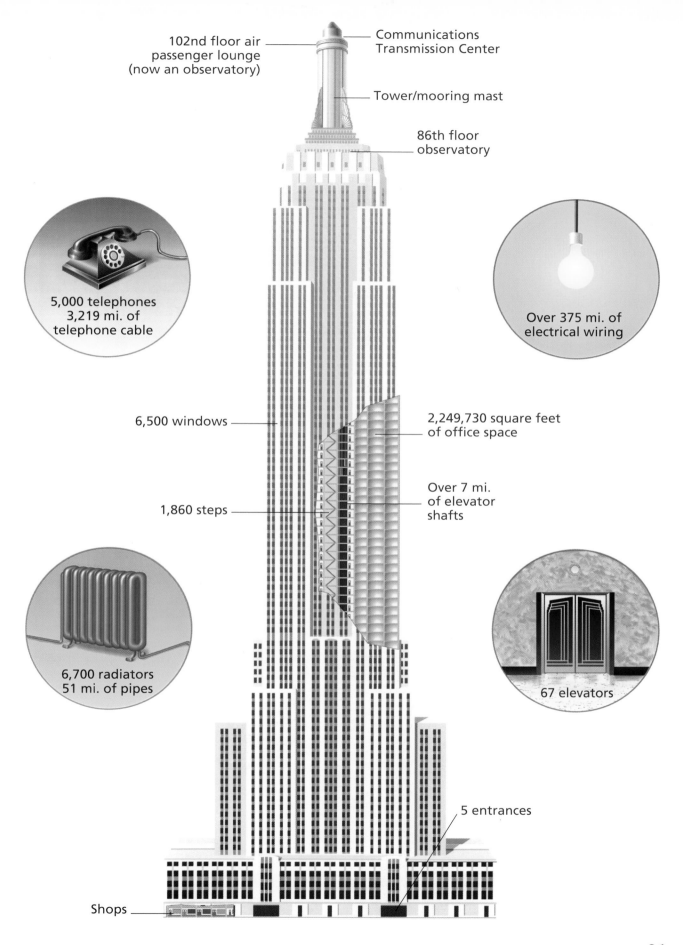

102nd floor air passenger lounge (now an observatory)

Communications Transmission Center

Tower/mooring mast

86th floor observatory

5,000 telephones 3,219 mi. of telephone cable

Over 375 mi. of electrical wiring

6,500 windows

2,249,730 square feet of office space

1,860 steps

Over 7 mi. of elevator shafts

6,700 radiators 51 mi. of pipes

67 elevators

5 entrances

Shops

CHAPTER FIVE

OPEN FOR BUSINESS

On May 1, 1931, at 11:15 A.M., Al Smith gave his grandchildren the word: "All right, kids, get to it!" They needed his help to cut the red, white, and blue ribbon across the main entrance of the building, but then the Empire State Building was officially open.

Smith and his family were joined by 350 guests, while police and state troopers kept the crowds of onlookers out on the street. At 11:30 A.M., President Herbert Hoover

◀ Smith, accompanied by his family and friends, in the lobby on opening day. Standing in front of a stainless-steel relief of the building, they posed for photographers.

◄ One of the guests on opening day was the governor of New York, Franklin Delano Roosevelt, a future president of the United States. He can be seen here on the 86th floor observation deck with ex-governor Al Smith.

▼ The front page of the *New York Times* on May 2, 1931, the day after the Empire State Building opened.

pressed a button from the White House in Washington, D.C. The lights went on in the lobby of the tallest building in the world.

The architect William Lamb had sailed for Europe to avoid all the opening day fuss. He sent a message from his ship: "One day out and I can still see the building."

The New York Times

Copyright, 1931, by The New York Times Company.

NEW YORK, SATURDAY, MAY 2, 1931.

WASHINGTON IS COOL TO ANY WORLD MOVE ON DEBTS OR TARIFF

Hint Precedes the Discussions Scheduled by International Chamber at the Capital.

HAS DAMPENING TENDENCY

Some Delegations Pinned Hope on Sessions to Start Action, Leading to Changes.

HOOVER WORKS ON SPEECH

He Will Deliver Address to the Business Congress at the Opening Monday Morning.

Di Robilant's Aide Dies of Jungle Fever; Italian Aviator Is Recovering in Brazil

Wireless to The New York Times.

SAO PAULO, May 1.—A telegram received at Sao Paulo late today advised the Italian Consul that Mauranta Quarenta, mechanic of Count di Robilant's plane, died at San José this morning from injuries and exhaustion. Count di Robilant, occupying the next bed, when informed of Signor Quarenta's death shortly before noon, at first refused to believe it. Later he developed a high fever, causing considerable alarm. The hospital doctors now fear Count di Robilant may be suffering from a tropical fever contracted during his eighteen days of wandering, after the crash of his plane.

The Italian Consul at Sao Paulo informed Signor Quarenta's family, living at Rio de Janeiro, of his death and the Italian Government will transport the family to Italy.

Count di Robilant is unable to see visitors and the hospital doctors here advised the Vice Consul at Sao Paulo that he will be transported tomorrow morning to Assis, where better medical assistance is obtainable. He is

believed to be out of danger, but requires special treatment.

The dispatches are being received here from Porto Presidente Epitacio, which is the nearest town to San José having telegraph connections. It takes half a day even for messages to come through from there.

Signor Quarenta died as the result of yellow fever contracted on the tortuous walk through dense forests, it is reported. Count di Robilant, although also affected, is expected to regain his health soon.

When Count di Robilant left Sao Paulo he followed the wrong route, due to a storm, for two hours. Then he flew three hours without knowing his whereabouts or direction. Aviation experts declare that because of the flier's great skill in landing in the dense forest he saved the plane from destruction.

A cablegram was received by the Italian Vice Consul here today from Count di Robilant's brother, living in New York requesting information about the flier.

EMPIRE STATE TOWER TALLEST IN WORLD IS OPENED BY HOOVER

President Presses Button in Washington, Lighting Up 1,250-Foot Building.

HE CONGRATULATES SMITH

Governor and Mayor Praise Vision and Courage of Leader in Project.

THOUSANDS SEE CEREMONY

Grandchildren of Ex-Governor Pull Ribbons at Entrance—Notables Inspect Structure.

Gives Hope
t Believed Lost

New York Times.
Congo, May 1.—
nce, leader of an
e Belgian Congo,
24 and proceeded
ril 29. No one
anything special
party.

as believed by his
Victor Torrance
to have been
April 28 after a
his camp in the
ss. Captain Tor-
so notified by a
rom the wilder-
runner and sent
dison, a member

authority on the
a party of ten
er white men and
medico-scientific
sponsored by a
k business men.

TS MOVE
SBON RULE

33

"This reminds me of home. We have white elephants too."

King Prajadhipok of Siam, visiting the Empire State Building in 1931

Public reaction to the Empire State Building was favorable, and it immediately won awards from architectural organizations. In spite of this, its offices were slow to fill up with renters during the Great Depression, with under half of the space rented on opening day. It took ten more years to let the rest, and the building became known by some as the "Empty" State Building. However, the building was far from empty. From the beginning, it was crowded with tourists who rode up in the elevators to the observation deck on the 86th floor.

▶ In 1934, during the Depression, tourists at the Empire State Building were cheered by the sight of this team of acrobats, seen balanced on the ledge of the 86th floor observation deck.

The Great Depression (1929–39)

The poverty cycle continued through the decade. The worst year was 1933, with a quarter of the workforce unemployed. Just when it looked as though things couldn't get any worse, severe drought brought devastation to the midwest of the United States, as seen in this picture taken in 1936. The machinery on this abandoned South Dakota farm was buried in dust as once-productive farmland became part of the Dust Bowl.

Some exciting businesses did move in early on. The NBC televison company made its first broadcast from a television station atop the Empire State Building on December 22, 1931. Television was still experimental, and NBC didn't begin operating the first commercial TV station until almost a decade later. Radio broadcasts had started when the building opened, coming from the rooftop Communications Transmission Center.

◀ In the early 1930s, the General Electric company installed a 59-foot-high rod on the top of the building, in order to do research into lightning. The rod was repeatedly jolted by lightning bolts, but the current passed safely through the building's steel frame and into the ground.

In the 1930s airships, rather than airplanes, were seen as the coming form of transportation between Europe and the United States. John Raskob had insisted that the architects design the Empire State Building tower as a mooring mast for airships. Engineers told him this was impossible, because the windy updrafts caused by tall buildings would make it dangerous to land. But Raskob wouldn't listen.

In September 1931, a small airship managed to moor for three minutes before the updraft became too perilous. The U.S. Navy made a second try two weeks later, but their airship almost turned over, nearly sweeping spectators from the tower. Finally, Raskob understood that the mooring mast would not work.

▼ Airships fly over the Empire State Building in 1931, but do not attempt to land. Although airships were making transatlantic flights at the time, they were soon to be replaced by passenger airplanes.

There was a more serious aviation accident at the Empire State Building some years later. On July 28, 1945, a U.S. Army bomber plane lost its way in the fog and flew into the 78th and 79th floor, exploding in flames. The pilot, his two passengers, and eleven other people were killed. The Empire State Building rocked twice and settled. There was a jagged hole in the side of building, and one of the massive steel beams was bent, but the structure was otherwise unharmed.

"There were flames from the top of the building down to the 20th floor. Pieces started shattering down. I watched the flames rip through the building."

Lieutenant Frank Covey, an eyewitness to the airplane crash in 1945

◄ This photograph shows where the B-25 bomber crashed into the Empire State Building. Part of the airplane's wreckage can be seen hanging from the 78th floor.

The Depression was finally ended by World War II (1939–1945). When the United States entered the war in 1941, millions of people went into the army, and millions more found jobs making ammunition, clothing, and equipment for the armed forces. For the first time in the history of the country, women went to work in record numbers.

▼ Bombers fly over New York at the beginning of World War II. Wartime in the city meant the return of prosperity, bringing about the end of mass unemployment.

After the war, with the economy growing again, the Empire State Building came into its own as a center for communications. Many communication "firsts" have come from the Empire State Building. The world's most powerful, far-reaching television tower was placed on top of the building on December 1, 1950. In 1965, the most powerful Master FM radio antenna system in the world was added.

▶ Equipped with its own lightning rod and aircraft warning lights, the present television antenna has given the Empire State Building an overall height of 1,453 ft. (443 m).

▼ A worker in 1950 installing the television tower, which was constructed from 60 tons of steel

Many radio and television stations still broadcast from the Empire State Building, and the building also transmits for the New York Telephone Company. It provides paging services, microwave operations, TV relay services, and two-way radio facilities. The ever-advancing technology of the building reflects the huge changes that have been made this century in the world's communications.

The Empire State Building has always provided entertainment as well as communication. It has appeared in over 90 movies since King Kong fell from the tower and has traditionally attracted many contests and stunts. Since 1932, people have raced up the building's 1,860 steps. The fastest climb recorded was in 1993, at ten minutes and eighteen seconds.

▲ A recent movie of Roald Dahl's famous story, *James and the Giant Peach*, features the Empire State Building in a dramatic moment, as the peach lands on the top and is spiked by the mast.

The observatories, visited yearly by over 3.5 million people, are often the sites of romantic meetings. However, there is so much buildup of static electricity on top of the building that people who kiss there have sometimes found their embrace electrically charged!

SOUVENIR OF VISIT TO THE MOST FAMOUS BUILDING IN THE WORLD

EMPIRE STATE OBSERVATORIES

1263000

◀ Tourists on the 86th floor observation deck can get a marvelous view of New York City and beyond.

The *Daily Mail* Transatlantic Air Race, from London's Post Office Tower (now the British Telecom Tower) to the Empire State Building, was won in 1969 by Clement Freud. It took him eight hours, four minutes, and eighteen seconds. The race commemorated the world's first transatlantic flight fifty years before.

The building has two annual camp-outs, one in November for Boy Scouts and one in March for Girl Scouts. At sunrise on Easter Sunday, New Yorkers can attend a religious service at the top of the building.

The Empire State Building now houses about 650 different companies, including the Guinness World of Records, and about 20,000 people work there. About 250 people help to run and maintain the actual building. The building has banks, a post office, restaurants, bars, hairdressers, and stores of all kinds.

In 1986 the Empire State Building became a National Historic Landmark, which means it can't be torn down because it is an important part of the city's history. For 41 years, it remained the tallest building in the world. In 1972, it was topped by the twin towers of the World Trade Center in lower Manhattan, and in 1974 by the Sears Tower in Chicago. Not to be defeated, in the 1970s Shreve, Lamb, and Harmon came up with some designs for replacing the top 21 floors of the Empire State Building with a modern, 33-floor structure. Luckily, the plans never made it beyond the drawing board!

Now the Petronas Towers in Malaysia have taken the title of the world's tallest building away from the United States, having reached 1,482 ft. (452 m). By the year 2000, even they may well be eclipsed by China's World Financial Center in Shanghai, at 1,499 ft. (457 m). For most people, however, the Empire State Building remains the world's definitive skyscraper.

▲ The Petronas Towers in Kuala Lumpur, Malaysia, seen here under construction in 1996, are the world's tallest buildings— for the moment.

◄ Since 1976, the top of the Empire State Building has been lit in different colors to honor many different occasions, showing blue and white for the Yankees during baseball season, and red and green for Christmas. The lights are turned off on foggy nights during the migrating seasons, so birds won't be confused and fly into the building.

43

TIME LINE

1700–1899

1789 George Washington inaugurated in New York as president of the United States of America

1799 Farmer John Thompson buys the future site of the Empire State Building from the City of New York

1827 William B. Astor buys site for $20,500

1865 Henry Bessemer perfects open-hearth process of making steel from iron and other elements

1885 W. L. Jenney's Home Insurance Building constructed with Bessemer-steel beams in Chicago

1900–29

1914 Woolworth Building completed

1920 Nationwide Prohibition begins in United States

1928 Waldorf-Astoria Hotel sold for $16 million to John J. Raskob and partners

1929 The company of Empire State Inc. is formed

October: Demolition of the Waldorf-Astoria Hotel begins

October 24: Wall Street Crash

1930–39

1930 Chrysler Building completed

January: Excavation begins at Empire State Building site

March: Construction of Empire State Building begins

September: Cornerstone laid by Alfred E. Smith

1931 May 1: Empire State Building opens and radio broadcasts from building start

December 22: First television transmission from top of Empire State Building

1932 First footrace up 1,860 steps of Empire State Building

1933 Empire State Building stars in the movie *King Kong*

1939 World War II begins

1940–1969

1945 World War II ends

1945 July 28: airplane crashes into side of Empire State Building, killing 14 people

1948 Hundreds of birds crash into tower during migration

1950 Television tower installed on Empire State Building

1965 FM radio antenna added to top of Empire State Building

1969 Transatlantic Air Race from Post Office Tower in London to Empire State Building

1970–1996

1972 Towers of World Trade Center in New York become world's tallest buildings

1974 Sears Tower in Chicago becomes world's tallest building

1976 Ticket sold to Empire State Building's 50-millionth visitor

1986 Empire State Building declared an historic landmark

1996 Petronas Towers in Malaysia become world's tallest buildings

GLOSSARY

Airship
A passenger carrier held up by a gas-filled balloon.

Architect
The person who designs a building or structure.

Communications
Ways of transmitting information, including computer networks, television, radio, telephones, and postal services.

Derrick
A machine for moving and lifting heavy weights, with an adjustable arm attached to the base of the main post.

Excavation
Digging into the earth, usually to make a foundation for a building.

I-beam
A metal beam that, when seen from the top or bottom, looks like the capital letter I. The most important beam used in the construction of the Empire State Building, its shape makes the beam very strong.

Immigrant
A person who comes to live in a country from abroad.

Marble
A hard stone formed naturally from limestone or dolomite, usually with more than one color in striped or swirling patterns.

Perpendicular
Going straight up, at right angles to the base.

Quarry
An open pit from which stone is dug, cut, or blasted free.

Rivet
A metal bolt with a head on one end that goes through two beams or other parts and joins them together. The metal is fused from the heat of the rivet, and the "headless" end is then pounded to form a second head.

Steel
A hard, strong alloy of iron and carbon used as a building material.

Stocks
Shares giving part ownership in a company. Stocks are sold to raise money for the business. If the business makes money, stockholders then receive dividends. They also have voting rights on some decisions about the company.

FURTHER INFORMATION

BOOKS

Brown, David. *The Random House Book of How Things Were Built*. New York: Random House, 1992.

Dunn, Andrew. *Skyscrapers*. Structures. New York: Thomson Learning, 1993.

Macaulay, David. *Unbuilding*. Boston: Houghton Mifflin, 1980.

Oxlade, Chris. *Skyscrapers and Towers*. Austin, TX: Raintree Steck-Vaughn, 1997.

Richardson, Joy. *Skyscrapers*. Picture Science. New York: Facts on File, 1994.

Sauvain, Philip. *Skyscrapers*. How We Build. Ada, OK: Garrett Educational Corp., 1990.

Tauranac, John. *The Empire State Building*. New York: Scribner's, 1995.

Picture acknowledgments

The publishers would like to thank the following for allowing their pictures to be reproduced: Avery Architectural and Fine Arts Library, Columbia University in the City of New York: page 18 (left), 22, 26 (left*); Copyright © 1929/1931 by the New York Times Co (reprinted by permission): pages 17, 33; Corbis-Bettmann/AFP: page 41 (top); Corbis-Bettmann/UPI: pages 16, 23, 27, 32, 33, 34, 37; Corbis-Bettmann: pages 10, 13 (top right), 17 (top); Empire State Building, managed by Helmsley-Spear, Inc: pages 1, 3, 12–13, 25, 30, 44, 45; Guild Entertainment: page 40; Peter Newark's American Pictures: pages 4-5, 6, 7 (bottom left), 8, 9 (right), 11, 20, 21, 24 (both*), 26 (right*), 28*, 29 (right*), 35 (top); Photri, Inc: pages 4 (left), 9 (left), 18 (right), 35 (bottom), 36, 38 (left), 38 (right) (Ray Corbett), 41 (B Kulik); Tony Stone Images: front cover (Fred George), pages 15 (left),15 (right) (Joseph Pobereskin), 29 (left) (Chris Hunt), 39 (A and L Sinibaldi), 42–43 (Cosmo Condina); Superstock: page 19 (R King).

The pictures above marked * were taken by Lewis Hine (1874–1940), who was commissioned to photograph the construction of the Empire State Building. He performed some daring feats to take these wonderful photographs of the equally brave men who worked on the building.

INDEX